HOLLY JOLLY
ORNAMENTAL APPLIQUÉ

Becky Campbell

American Quilter's Society
www.AmericanQuilter.com

The American Quilter's Society or AQS is dedicated to quilting excellence. AQS promotes the triumphs of today's quilter, while remaining dedicated to the quilting tradition. AQS believes in the promotion of this art and craft through AQS Publishing and AQS QuiltWeek®.

DIRECTOR OF PUBLICATIONS: KIMBERLY HOLLAND TETREV
ASSISTANT EDITOR: ADRIANA FITCH
PROOFING EDITOR: CAITLIN TETREV
ILLUSTRATIONS: BECKY CAMPBELL
GRAPHIC DESIGN: SARAH BOZONE
COVER DESIGN: MICHAEL BUCKINGHAM
QUILT PHOTOGRAPHY: CHARLES R. LYNCH

Additional copies of this book may be ordered from the American Quilter's Society, PO Box 3290, Paducah, KY 42002-3290, or online at www.ShopAQS.com.

Attention Photocopying Service: Please note the following— Publisher and author give permission to print pages 11-58 and 61-62.

Text and Illustrations © 2015, Author, Becky Campbell
Artwork © 2015, American Quilter's Society

American Quilter's Society
www.AmericanQuilter.com

Library of Congress Cataloging-in-Publication Data

Names: Campbell, Becky (Writer on quilting), author.
Title: Holly jolly ornamental appliqué / By Becky Campbell.
Description: Paducah, KY : American Quilter's Society, 2015.
Identifiers: LCCN 2015043271 | ISBN 9781604604009 (pbk.)
Subjects: LCSH: Patchwork--Patterns. | Quilting--Patterns. | Appliqué--Patterns. | Christmas decorations.
Classification: LCC TT835 .C3564 2015 | DDC 746.46--dc23
LC record available at http://lccn.loc.gov/2015043271

Contents

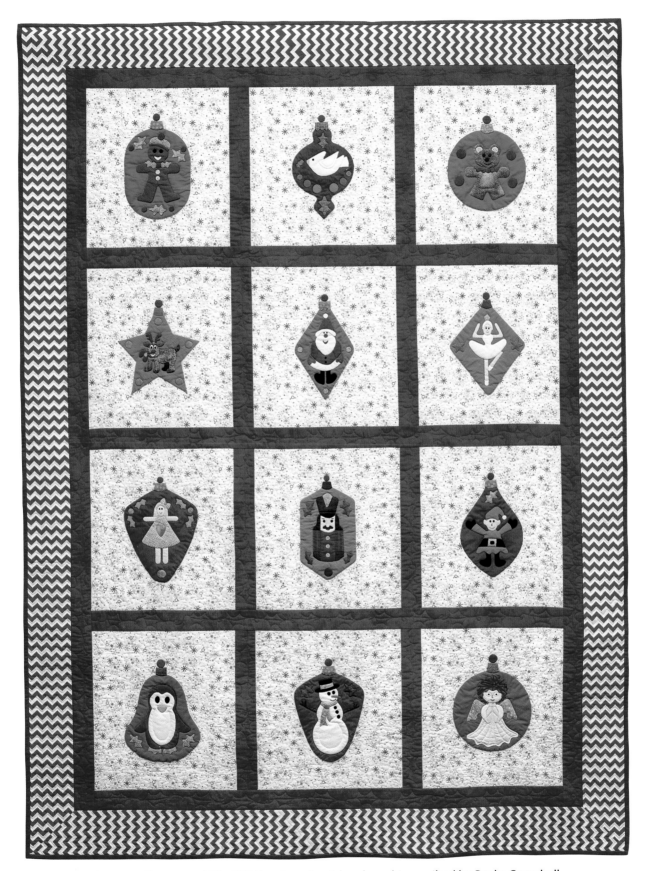

CHRISTMAS COLLECTION, 59" x 79". Hand appliquéd and machine quilted by Becky Campbell.

Fabric Requirements

The measurements are detailed so you can make alternative fabric choices and know how allowances have been calculated.

Block Fabric - 2¾ yards

(12) blocks 15½" x 16½", includes 1" allowance for trimming blocks once the appliqué is complete.

40" (Fabric Width) ÷ 16½" =
2 blocks per WOF

(12) blocks ÷ 2 blocks per cut = (6) 16½" cuts =
99" ÷ 36" (1 yard) = 2.75 yards

Sashing Fabric - 1 yard

(13) 2 ½" WOF strips =
32½" round up to 36" = 1 yard

Border - 1½ yards

(10) 5" WOF strips = 50" ÷ 36"
(1 yard) = 1.38 yards (round up)
54" = 1 ½ yards

Backing - 4 yards

59" + 8" for extra allowance
when quilting = 67" x 2 seam
will be lengthwise = 134" ÷ 36"
(1 yard) = 3.72 round up to 4 yards

Binding - ¾ yard

(8) 2 ½" WOF strips = 20" ÷ 36"
(1 yard) = .55 yard, round up to ¾ yards

Appliqué Fabrics

Various amounts of multiple colors

Product Supplies

C Jenkins™–8½" x 11" freezer paper sheets, creates templates.

Perfect Piecing by June Tailor®–printable transparent foundation sheets, create a placement guide.

Print n' Fuse™–for the trapunto affect or fusible appliqué.

Roxanne's Glue Baste-It–a temporary basting glue. The accordian style bottle is easier to apply and the application tip does not dry up.

Clover® 482/W Seam Ripper or Pointed Tool–to turn down the cut edge of appliqué.

Needle–your choice.

Thimble–your choice.

OLFA® Rotary Mat–(6" x 8") creates a good surface to work on.

Karen Kay Buckley's Perfect Scissors (Large)–to cut out appliqué shapes.

Christmas Collection Construction

Finished Size 59" x 79"

General Information (All seam allowances are ¼")

Blocks
Cut (12) blocks 15½" x 16½". After appliqué is complete, trim to 14½" x 15½" to clean up the edges.

Sashing
Cut (3) 2½" WOF (width of fabric) strips for sashing between blocks.
Subcut (8) 2½" x 15½" strips. Stitch one strip between blocks 1 and 2. Repeat this step between blocks 2 and 3, blocks 4 and 5, blocks 5 and 6, blocks 7 and 8, blocks 8 and 9, blocks 10 and 11 and blocks 11 and 12. This creates 4 rows.

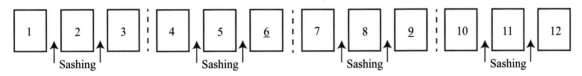

Cut (6) 2½" WOF strips. Piece strips together to equal (5) 46½" or the width of the rows you just created. Stitch one strip to the top and one strip to the bottom of row 1, add row 2. Stitch one strip to the top and bottom of row 3, stitch to the previous section. Stitch one strip to the bottom of row 4 and add to the previous section.

Cut (4) 2½" WOF strips. Piece strips together to equal (2) 70½" or the length measurement of the rows joined.
Stitch one strip to the left and one to the right side of the project.

Border
Cut (10) 5" WOF strips. Piece strips to equal (2) 62½" or the width measurement of the quilt, or 74½" if mitering. Stitch one strip to the top and one to the bottom.

Piece the remaining strips to equal (2) 80" strips or the length measurement of the quilt or (2) 92" strips, extra allowance if mitering. Stitch one strip to the left and one strip to the right side of the quilt.

Trapunto without stuffing
This is the time to apply the Print n' Fuse batted shapes to the wrong side of the background fabric, matching the shapes with the corresponding appliqué shape. Remove the paper and iron one shape at a time. This prevents the shapes from shifting and being ironed in the wrong place. Now sandwich the quilt: front, batting and back.

Quilt
Quilt as desired. Once the overall quilting is complete, stitch in the ditch around each batted shape. Match the thread color to the fabric you are stitching on and turn the stitch length down one notch.

Binding
Cut (8) 2½" WOF strips, piece strips together to equal 280", that measurement allows for 10" to join the ends together. Fold binding in half lengthwise and press.

Apply binding and add a label to identify your work. Great Job!

Innovative Appliqué

Specific brands are recommended because their performance is superior.

Turned Edge Appliqué Directions

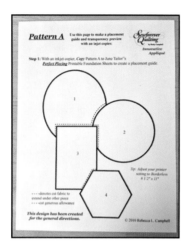

Fig. 1

Fig. 2

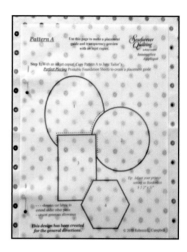

Fig. 3

Figs. 1-3. With an inkjet printer, copy Pattern A to Perfect Piecing to create a placement guide. Pin the placement to the front of the background fabric on the left side so it opens like a book. No tracing!

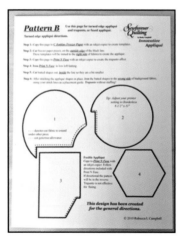

Fig. 4

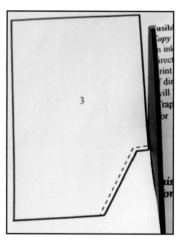

Fig. 5

Fig. 6

Figs. 4-6. With an inkjet printer, copy Pattern B onto C Jenkins Freezer Paper to create templates. Cut the freezer paper shapes on the outside of the black line, except at dashes. Leave the extra because that lays under another piece. No tracing!

| Fig. 7 | Fig. 8 | Fig. 9 |

Figs. 7-9. Iron to the right side of chosen fabrics. Cut ³⁄₁₆" around the template. Flip the piece over for the next step. Apply Roxanne's Glue Baste-It a bit inside the cut edge, and turn the cut edge of the fabric down into the glue. The freezer paper holds the shape and just the cut edge turns down.

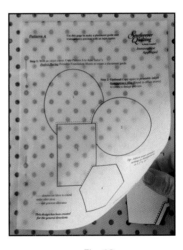

| Fig. 10 | Fig. 11 | Fig. 12 |

Figs. 10-12. Edges should be turned except at the dashes. Fig. 11 is the view from the right side. To place the shapes on the right side of the background fabric, apply Roxanne's glue to the wrong side of the piece around the perimeter, lift the placement guide and position in place. Allow the glue to dry for a second and then carefully remove the freezer paper.

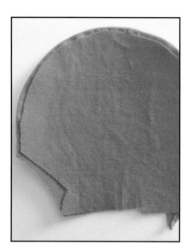

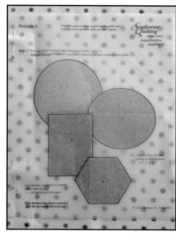

Fig. 13   Fig. 14   Fig. 15

Fig. 13. If the background fabric shows through the appliqué piece, line the piece with an extra layer of fabric. Fig. 14. This shows all the pieces glued in place with the freezer paper removed. Fig. 15. Remove placement guide to stitch by hand or machine.

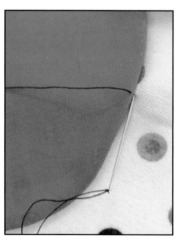

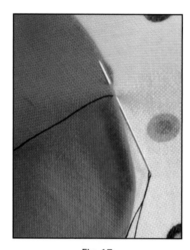

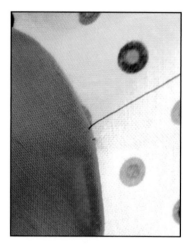

Fig. 16   Fig. 17   Fig. 18

Fig. 16. To hand stitch: Needle up into the folded edge of the appliqué piece, needle down straight out from where you came up and a little under the appliqué piece. Fig. 17. Needle up into the folded edge and repeat. Fig. 18. Use a color of thread that matches the appliqué piece, the stitches will disappear.

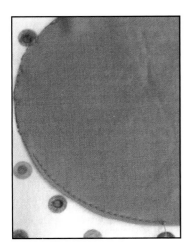

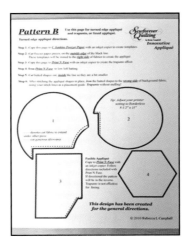

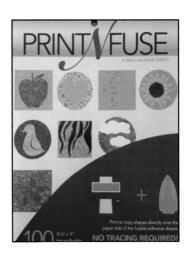

Fig. 19   Fig. 20   Fig. 21

Fig. 19. To machine stitch: Appliqué can be stitched with a variety of machine stitches. Figs. 20-21. To create trapunto without stuffing, copy Pattern B to Print n' Fuse with an inkjet printer.

Fusible Appliqué Directions

To make copies for fusible appliqué, use Pattern B, select the mirror image, reverse mode, or flip/horizontal on your printer's settings. Place Print n' Fuse in the printer tray so Pattern B prints on the paper side of Print n' Fuse.

Roughly cut the Print n' Fuse shapes beyond the lines, iron shapes to the wrong side of your chosen fabrics. Press for a few seconds with a hot dry iron. Let cool. Now cut out shapes on the solid black lines except at the dash lines. At the dash lines cut approximately ½" from the solid line to allow that area to extend under another piece.

Pin Pattern A Perfect Piecing placement guide to the right side of background fabric so it opens like a book. Remove the paper backing from cut shapes, lift the placement guide and slip the shapes under to place in the appropriate place. Iron shapes in place. Stitch in place with zigzag, satin or straight stitch.

Fig. 22

Fig. 23

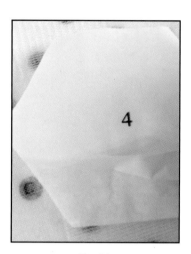

Fig. 24

Fig. 22. Iron the copy of Print n' Fuse to batting. Trapunto is best applied once the front of the quilt is assembled. Fig. 23. Cut inside the black line so the shape will fit inside the stitch lines on the wrong side of the background fabric. Fig. 24. Peel off the paper, flip the shape over, and iron in place using stitch lines on the wrong side of background fabric as placement.

Fig. 26

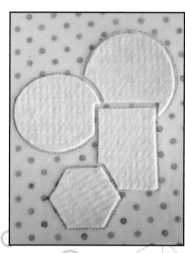

Fig. 25

Quilt as desired. Once the overall quilting is complete, turn your stitch length down to 2. Stitch in the ditch around the appliqué shapes, matching the thread color to the fabric you are stitching on. This locks the batted shapes in place and creates added dimension. Add the binding, a hanging sleeve, and your label.

Good job!

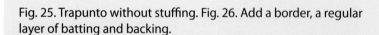

Fig. 25. Trapunto without stuffing. Fig. 26. Add a border, a regular layer of batting and backing.

Patterns

Angel

Angel

Angel: Pattern A

Copy this page to Perfect Piecing to make a placement guide (page 6).

This area gets tucked under the sides of her face.

Tip: Color small details with a Micron® Pigma pen. Pigma pens do not flow into the surrounding fabric. Perform this step before placing that piece on the background.

Tip: Adjust your printer setting to Borderless 8½" x 11".

© 2015 Rebecca L. Campbell

Angel: Pattern B

Copy this page for turned-edge appliqué
(page 8), trapunto (page 9), and fusible
appliqué (page 9).

------ denotes cutting a generous allowance
to extend under another piece.

2

1

ALL templates are shown at 100%.

Tip: Adjust your printer setting to
Borderless 8½" x 11".

Angel

Angel: Pattern B

Copy this page for turned-edge appliqué (page 8), trapunto (page 9), and fusible appliqué (page 9).

------ denotes cutting a generous allowance to extend under another piece.

Tip: Color small details with a Micron Pigma pen. Pigma pens do not flow into the surrounding fabric. Perform this step before placing that piece on the background.

Tip: Adjust your printer setting to Borderless 8½" x 11".

Ballerina

Ballerina

Ballerina: Pattern A

Copy this page to Perfect Piecing to make a placement guide (page 6).

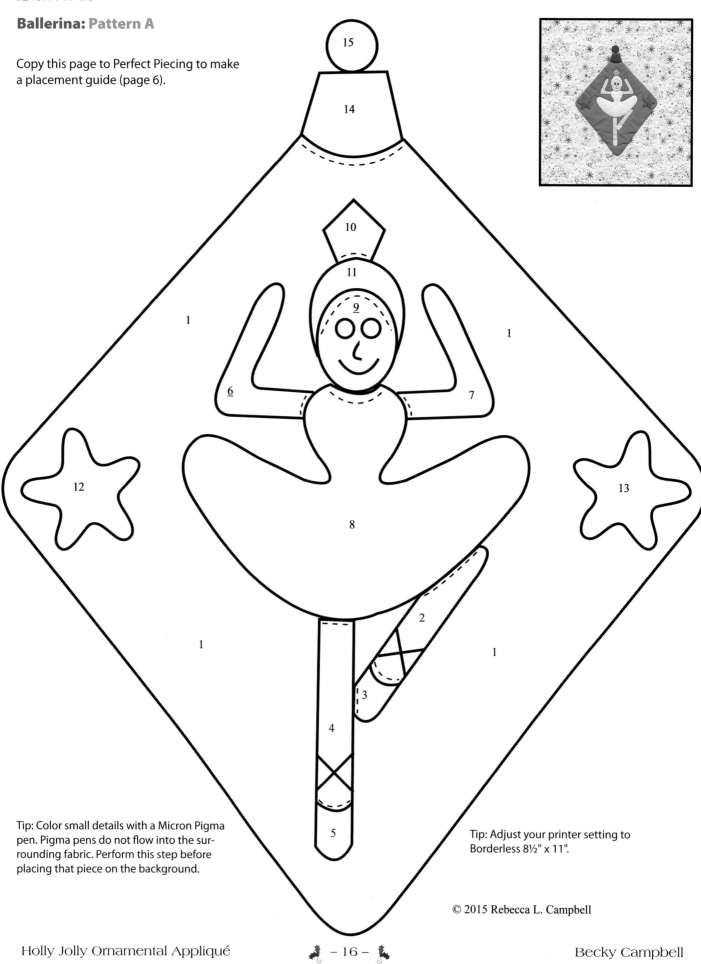

Tip: Color small details with a Micron Pigma pen. Pigma pens do not flow into the surrounding fabric. Perform this step before placing that piece on the background.

Tip: Adjust your printer setting to Borderless 8½" x 11".

© 2015 Rebecca L. Campbell

Ballerina: Pattern B

Copy this page for turned-edge appliqué
(page 8), trapunto (page 9), and fusible
appliqué (page 9).

------ denotes cutting a generous allowance
to extend under another piece.

Tip: Adjust your printer setting to
Borderless 8½" x 11".

Ballerina: Pattern B

Copy this page for turned-edge appliqué (page 8), trapunto (page 9), and fusible appliqué (page 9).

11

4

2

6

3

10

7

12

13

15

14

5

8

9

------ denotes cutting a generous allowance to extend under another piece.

Tip: Color small details with a Micron Pigma pen. Pigma pens do not flow into the surrounding fabric. Perform this step before placing that piece on the background.

Tip: Adjust your printer setting to Borderless 8½" x 11".

Bear

Bear

Bear: Pattern A

Copy this page to Perfect Piecing to make a placement guide (page 6).

Tip: Color small details with a Micron Pigma pen. Pigma pens do not flow into the surrounding fabric. Perform this step before placing that piece on the background.

Mouth line can be stitched with embroidery thread or drawn with permanent pen.

© 2015 Rebecca L. Campbell

Tip: Adjust your printer setting to Borderless 8½" x 11".

Bear: Pattern B

------ denotes cutting a generous allowance
to extend under another piece.

1

Copy this page for turned-edge appliqué
(page 8), trapunto (page 9), and fusible
appliqué (page 9).

Tip: Adjust your printer setting to
Borderless 8½" x 11".

Bear: Pattern B

Copy this page for turned-edge appliqué (page 8), trapunto (page 9), and fusible appliqué (page 9).

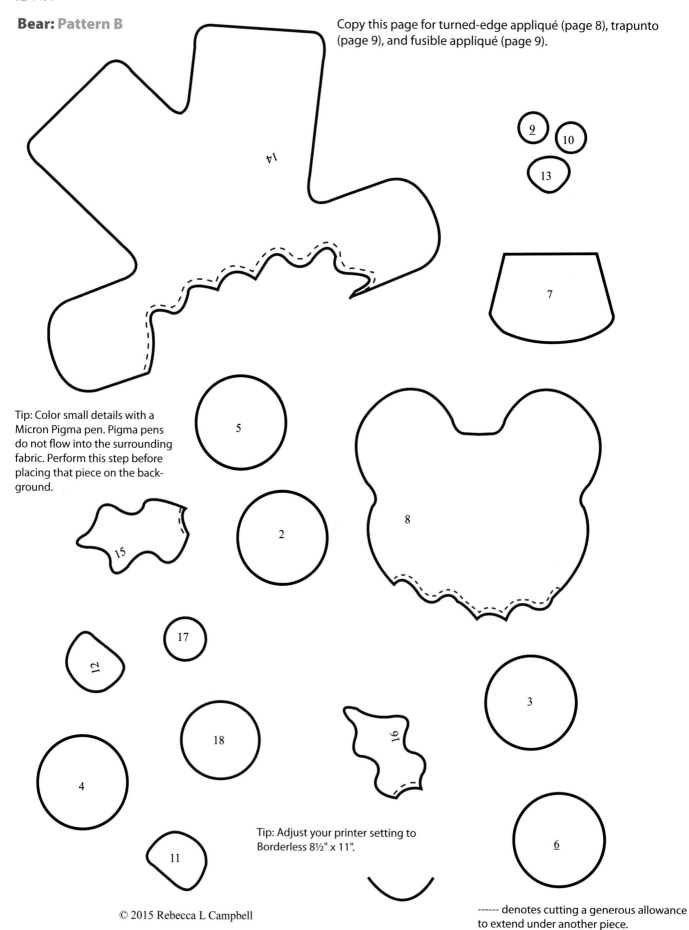

Tip: Color small details with a Micron Pigma pen. Pigma pens do not flow into the surrounding fabric. Perform this step before placing that piece on the background.

Tip: Adjust your printer setting to Borderless 8½" x 11".

------ denotes cutting a generous allowance to extend under another piece.

Holly Jolly Ornamental Appliqué

Becky Campbell

Clara

Clara

Clara: Pattern A

Copy this page to Perfect Piecing to make a placement guide (page 6).

Tip: Color small details with a Micron Pigma pen. Pigma pens do not flow into the surrounding fabric. Perform this step before placing that piece on the background.

Her face lays underneath her hair, her chin is turned and lays on top of the dress.

© 2015 Rebecca L. Campbell

Tip: Adjust your printer setting to Borderless 8½" x 11".

Holly Jolly Ornamental Appliqué   – 24 –   Becky Campbell

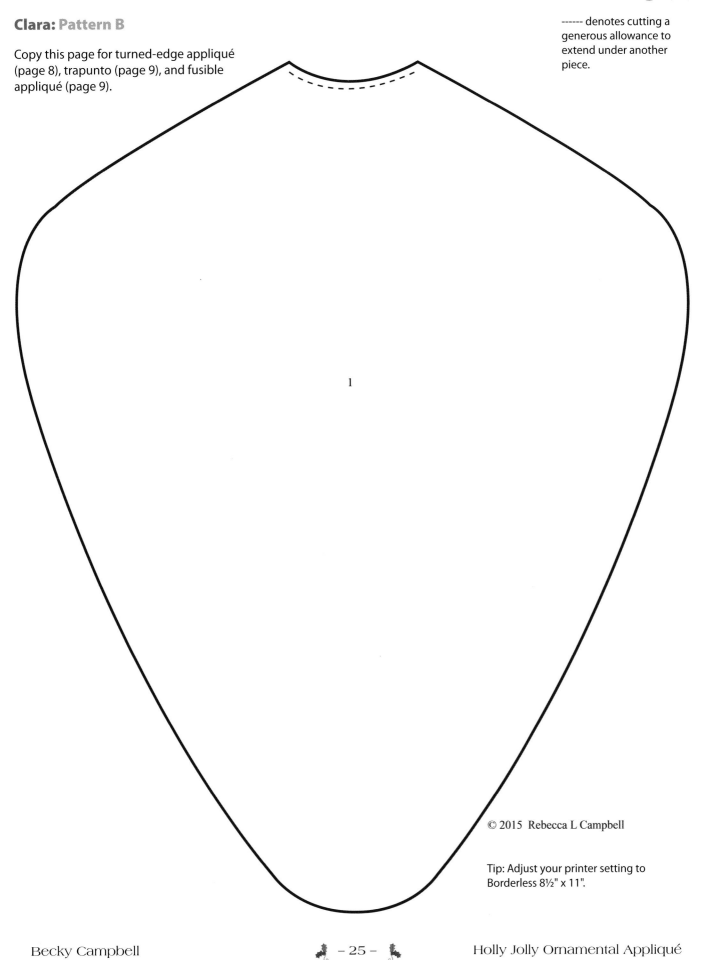

Clara: Pattern B

Copy this page for turned-edge appliqué
(page 8), trapunto (page 9), and fusible
appliqué (page 9).

------ denotes cutting a
generous allowance to
extend under another
piece.

Clara

1

© 2015 Rebecca L Campbell

Tip: Adjust your printer setting to
Borderless 8½" x 11".

Clara: Pattern B

Copy this page for turned-edge appliqué (page 8), trapunto (page 9), and fusible appliqué (page 9).

------ denotes cutting a generous allowance to extend under another piece.

Tip: Color small details with a Micron Pigma pen. Pigma pens do not flow into the surrounding fabric. Perform this step before placing that piece on the background.

Tip: Adjust your printer setting to Borderless 8½" x 11".

© 2015 Rebecca L Campbell

Dove

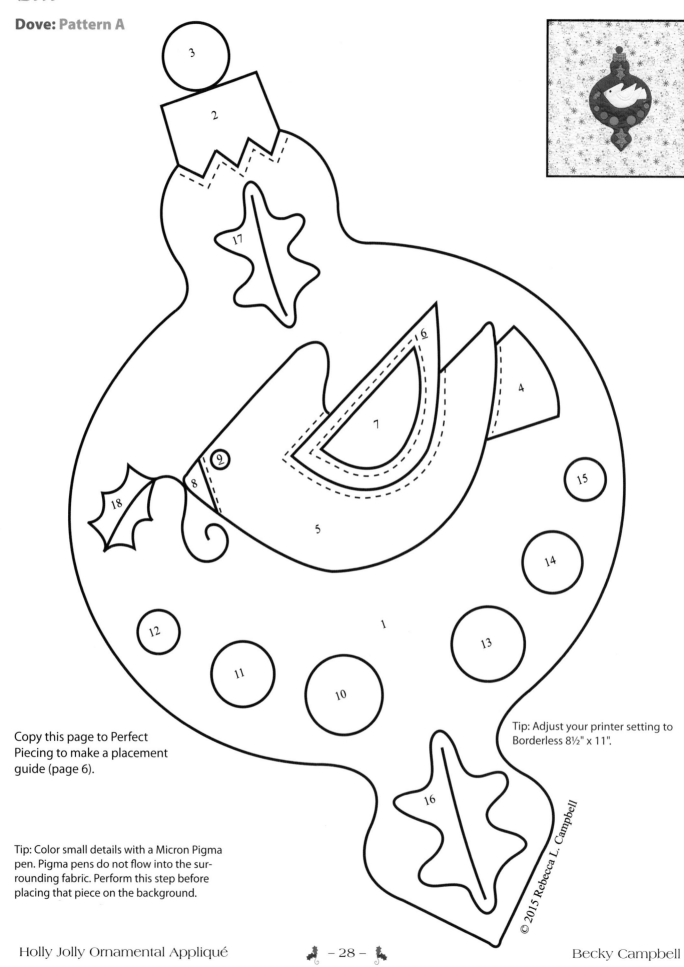

Copy this page to Perfect Piecing to make a placement guide (page 6).

Tip: Adjust your printer setting to Borderless 8½" x 11".

Tip: Color small details with a Micron Pigma pen. Pigma pens do not flow into the surrounding fabric. Perform this step before placing that piece on the background.

© 2015 Rebecca L. Campbell

Dove: Pattern B

Copy this page for turned-edge appliqué
(page 8), trapunto (page 9), and fusible
appliqué (page 9).

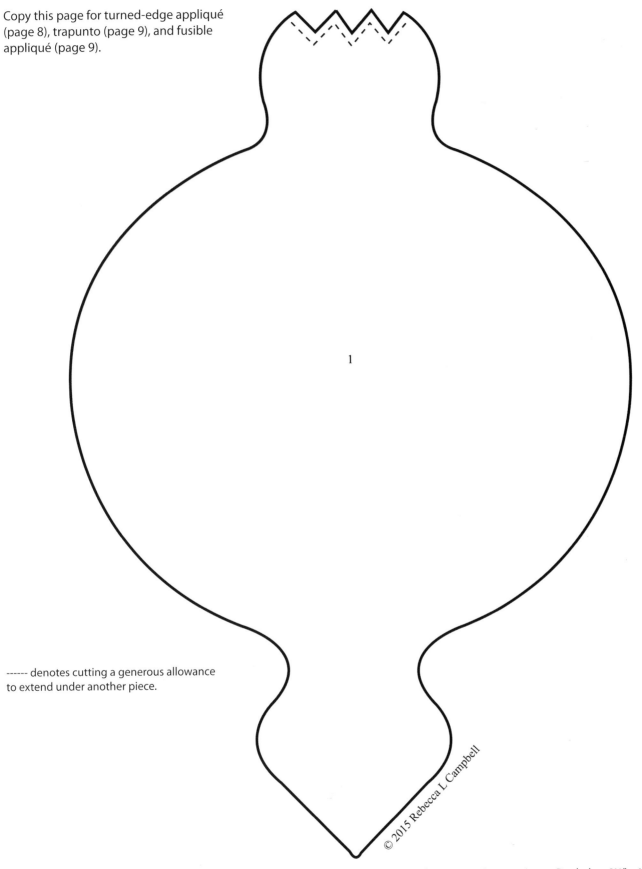

1

------ denotes cutting a generous allowance
to extend under another piece.

© 2015 Rebecca L Campbell

Tip: Adjust your printer setting to Borderless 8½" x 11".

Dove: Pattern B

Copy this page for turned-edge appliqué
(page 8), trapunto (page 9), and fusible
appliqué (page 9).

4

3

2

10

14

9

12   15

11

8

18

13

------ denotes cutting a generous allowance
to extend under another piece.

16

17

6

Tip: Color small details
with a Micron Pigma pen.
Pigma pens do not flow
into the surrounding
fabric. Perform this step
before placing that piece
on the background.

7

5

Tip: Adjust your printer setting to Borderless 8½" x 11".

Holly Jolly Ornamental Appliqué

Becky Campbell

Elf

Elf

Elf: Pattern A

Copy this page to
Perfect Piecing to
make a placement
guide (page 6).

Tip: Adjust your printer setting to
Borderless 8½" x 11".

Tip: Color small details with a Micron Pigma
pen. Pigma pens do not flow into the surrounding fabric. Perform this step before
placing that piece on the background.

© 2015 Rebecca L. Campbell

Elf: Pattern B

Copy this page for turned-edge appliqué
(page 8), trapunto (page 9), and fusible
appliqué (page 9).

------ denotes cutting a generous allowance
to extend under another piece.

Tip: Adjust your printer setting to
Borderless 8½" x 11".

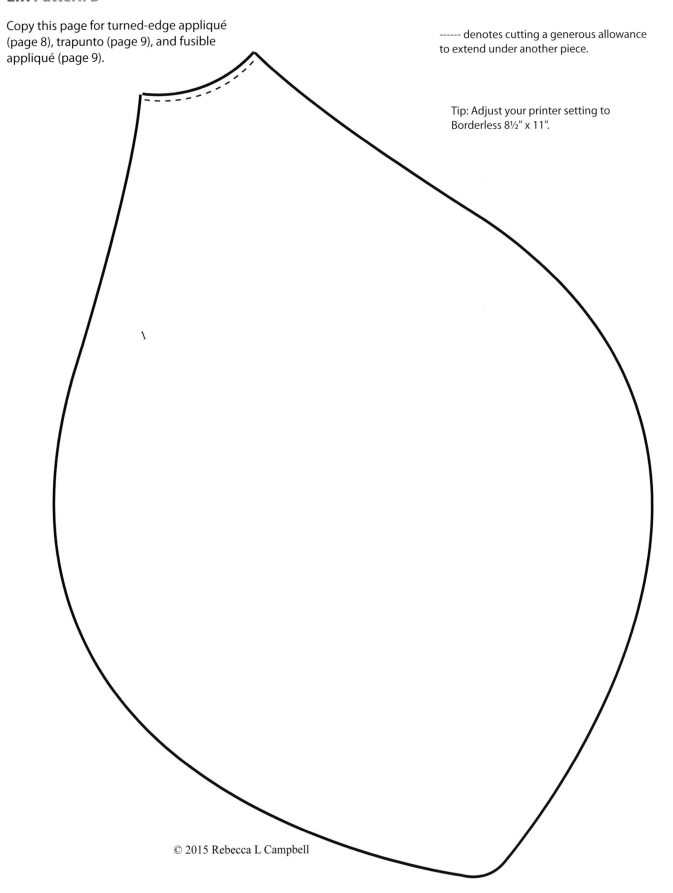

Elf: Pattern B

Copy this page for turned-edge appliqué
(page 8), trapunto (page 9), and fusible
appliqué (page 9).

------ denotes cutting a generous allowance
to extend under another piece.

8

12

3

Tip: Adjust your printer setting to
Borderless 8½" x 11".

Tip: Color small details with a Micron Pigma
pen. Pigma pens do not flow into the
surrounding fabric. Perform this step before
placing that piece on the background.

17

6

18

11

9

10

5

13

19

2

7

4

Gingerbread

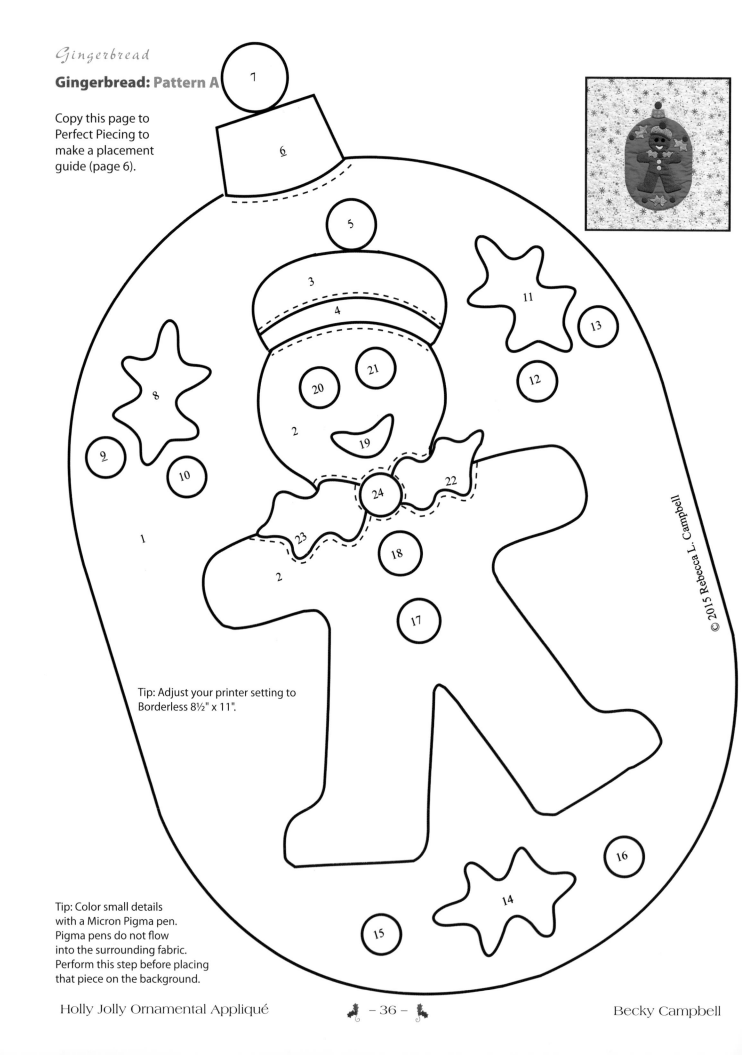

Gingerbread

Gingerbread: Pattern A

Copy this page to
Perfect Piecing to
make a placement
guide (page 6).

Tip: Adjust your printer setting to
Borderless 8½" x 11".

Tip: Color small details
with a Micron Pigma pen.
Pigma pens do not flow
into the surrounding fabric.
Perform this step before placing
that piece on the background.

© 2015 Rebecca L. Campbell

Gingerbread: Pattern B

Copy this page for turned-edge appliqué (page 8), trapunto (page 9), and fusible appliqué (page 9).

------ denotes cutting a generous allowance to extend under another piece.

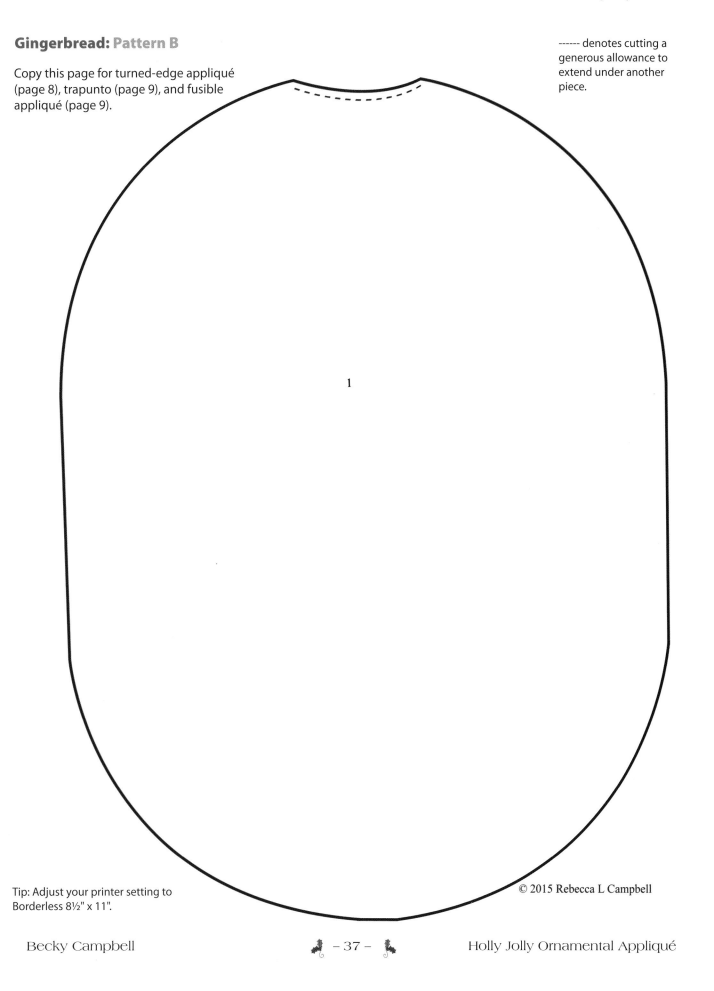

1

Tip: Adjust your printer setting to Borderless 8½" x 11".

© 2015 Rebecca L Campbell

Gingerbread: Pattern B

Copy this page for turned-edge appliqué (page 8), trapunto (page 9), and fusible appliqué (page 9).

------ denotes cutting a generous allowance to extend under another piece.

Tip: Color small details with a Micron Pigma pen. Pigma pens do not flow into the surrounding fabric. Perform this step before placing that piece on the background.

Tip: Adjust your printer setting to Borderless 8½" x 11".

© 2015 Rebecca L Campbell

Penguin

Penguin

Penguin: Pattern A

Copy this page to
Perfect Piecing to
make a placement
guide (page 6).

Tip: Color small details with a Micron
Pigma pen. Pigma pens do not flow
into the surrounding fabric. Perform
this step before placing that piece on
the background.

© 2015 Rebecca L. Campbell

Tip: Adjust your printer setting to
Borderless 8½" x 11".

Penguin: Pattern B

Copy this page for turned-edge appliqué
(page 8), trapunto (page 9), and fusible
appliqué (page 9).

Tip: Adjust your printer setting to Borderless 8½" x 11".

------ denotes cutting a generous allowance
to extend under another piece.

Penguin: Pattern B

Copy this page for turned-edge appliqué
(page 8), trapunto (page 9), and fusible
appliqué (page 9).

------ denotes cutting a
generous allowance to
extend under another
piece.

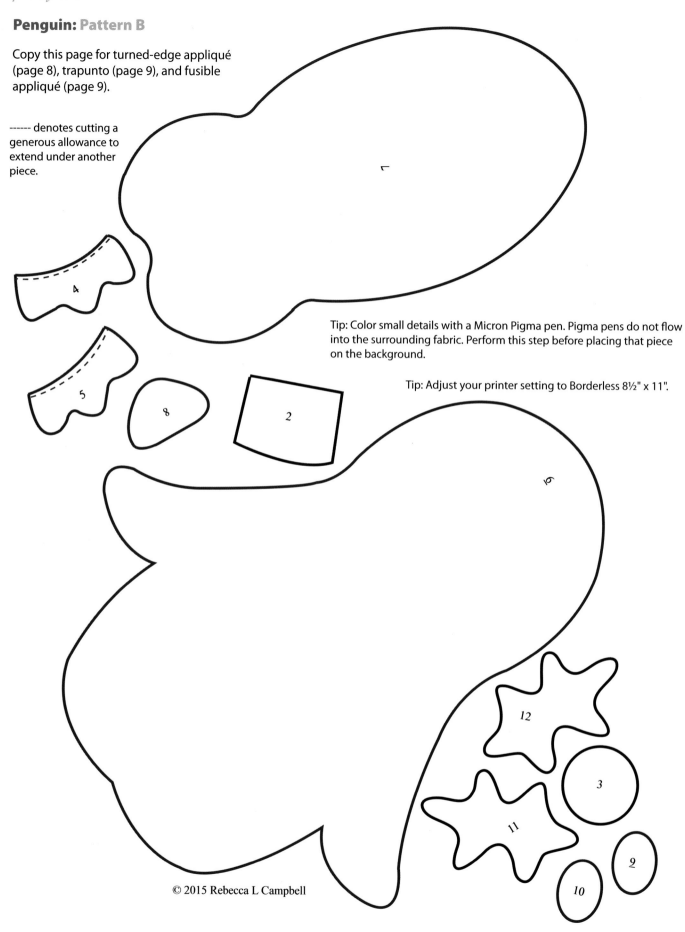

Tip: Color small details with a Micron Pigma pen. Pigma pens do not flow
into the surrounding fabric. Perform this step before placing that piece
on the background.

Tip: Adjust your printer setting to Borderless 8½" x 11".

© 2015 Rebecca L Campbell

Holly Jolly Ornamental Appliqué   – 42 –   Becky Campbell

Reindeer

Reindeer: Pattern A

Copy this page to Perfect Piecing to make a placement guide (page 6).

Tip: Color small details with a Micron Pigma pen. Pigma pens do not flow into the surrounding fabric. Perform this step before placing that piece on the background.

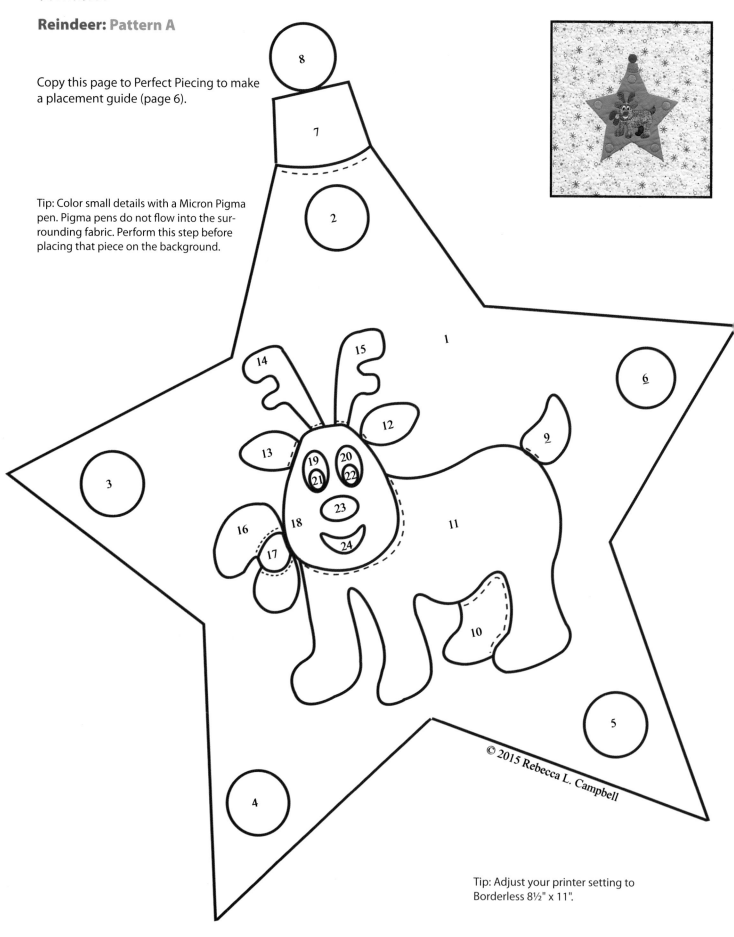

Tip: Adjust your printer setting to Borderless 8½" x 11".

Holly Jolly Ornamental Appliqué

Becky Campbell

Reindeer: Pattern B

Copy this page for turned-edge appliqué
(page 8), trapunto (page 9), and fusible
appliqué (page 9).

Tip: Adjust your printer setting to
Borderless 8½" x 11".

------ denotes cutting a generous allowance
to extend under another piece.

1

Reindeer: Pattern B

Copy this page for turned-edge appliqué
(page 8), trapunto (page 9), and fusible
appliqué (page 9).

Tip: Color small details with a Micron Pigma
pen. Pigma pens do not flow into the surrounding fabric. Perform this step before
placing that piece on the background.

Tip: Adjust your printer setting to
Borderless 8½" x 11".

------ denotes cutting a generous
allowance to extend under another
piece.

Santa

Santa: Pattern A

Copy this page to Perfect Piecing to make a placement guide (page 6).

3

2

17

15

16   12   23

1

14

13   9

19

8

21

18   10

4

22

11

7

5   6

Tip: Color small details with a Micron Pigma pen. Pigma pens do not flow into the surrounding fabric. Perform this step before placing that piece on the background.

© 2015 Rebecca L. Campbell

20

Tip: Adjust your printer setting to Borderless 8½" x 11".

Holly Jolly Ornamental Appliqué

Becky Campbell

Santa: Pattern B

Copy this page for turned-edge appliqué (page 8), trapunto (page 9), and fusible appliqué (page 9).

------ denotes cutting a generous allowance to extend under another piece.

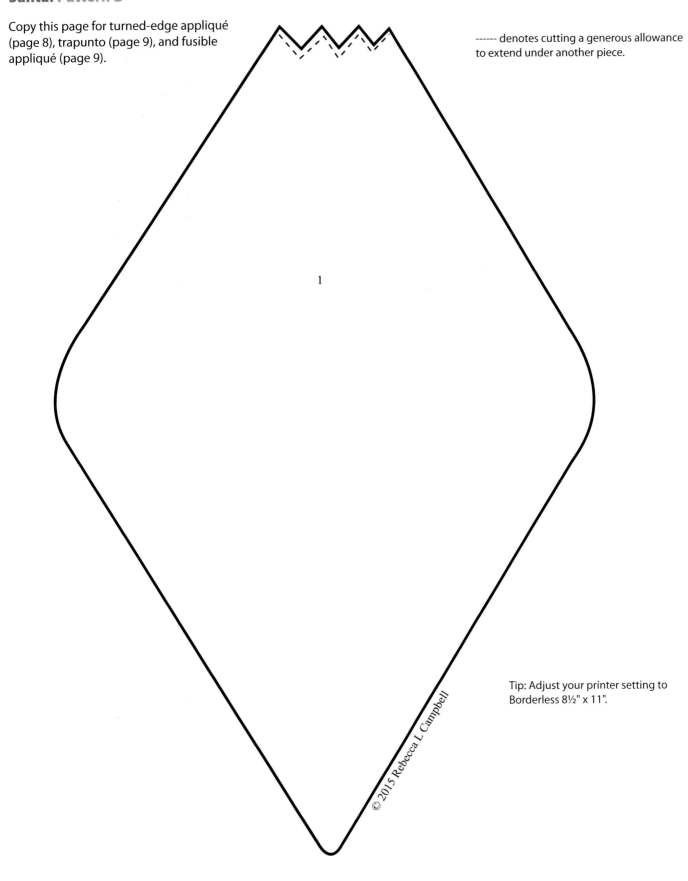

1

Tip: Adjust your printer setting to Borderless 8½" x 11".

© 2015 Rebecca L Campbell

Santa: Pattern B

Copy this page for turned-edge appliqué
(page 8), trapunto (page 9), and fusible
appliqué (page 9).

Tip: Adjust your printer setting to Borderless
8½" x 11".

Tip: Color small details with a Micron Pigma
pen. Pigma pens do not flow into the surrounding fabric. Perform this step before
placing that piece on the background.

------ denotes cutting a generous allowance
to extend under another piece.

© 2015 Rebecca L Campbell

Snowman

Snowman

Snowman: Pattern A

Copy this page to Perfect Piecing to make a place-ment guide (page 6).

Tip: Adjust your printer setting to Borderless 8½" x 11".

Tip: Color small details with a Micron Pigma pen. Pigma pens do not flow into the sur-rounding fabric. Perform this step before placing that piece on the background.

Snowman: Pattern B

Copy this page for turned-edge appliqué (page 8), trapunto (page 9), and fusible appliqué (page 9).

------ denotes cutting a generous allowance to extend under another piece.

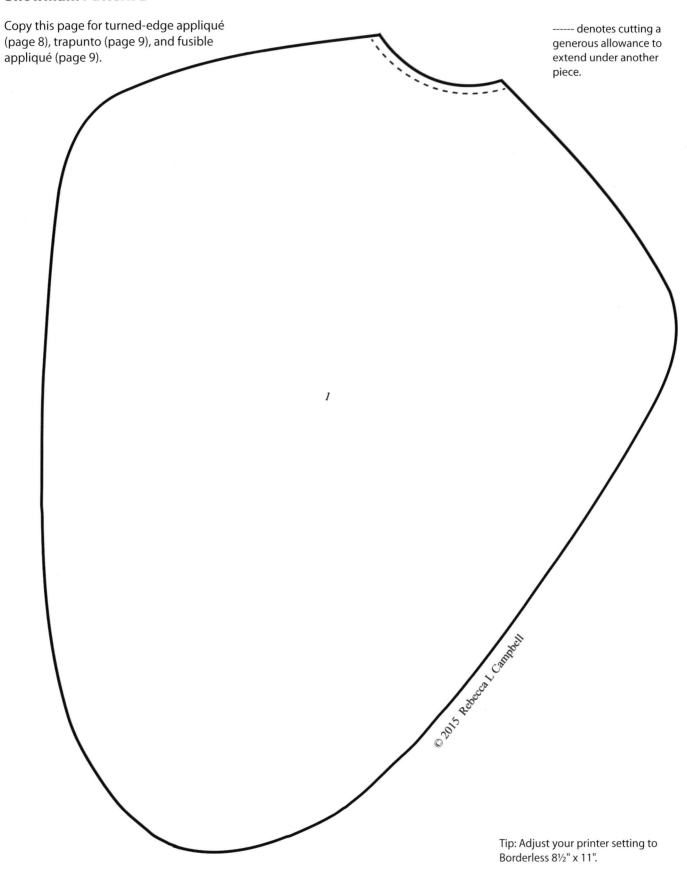

1

© 2015 Rebecca L Campbell

Tip: Adjust your printer setting to Borderless 8½" x 11".

Snowman: Pattern B

Copy this page for turned-edge appliqué
(page 8), trapunto (page 9), and fusible
appliqué (page 9).

------ denotes cutting a generous allowance
to extend under another piece.

© 2015 Rebecca L Campbell

Tip: Color small details with a Micron Pigma
pen. Pigma pens do not flow into the surrounding fabric. Perform this step before
placing that piece on the background.

Tip: Adjust your printer setting to
Borderless 8½" x 11".

Becky Campbell

Soldier

Soldier: Pattern A

Copy this page to
Perfect Piecing to
make a placement
guide (page 6).

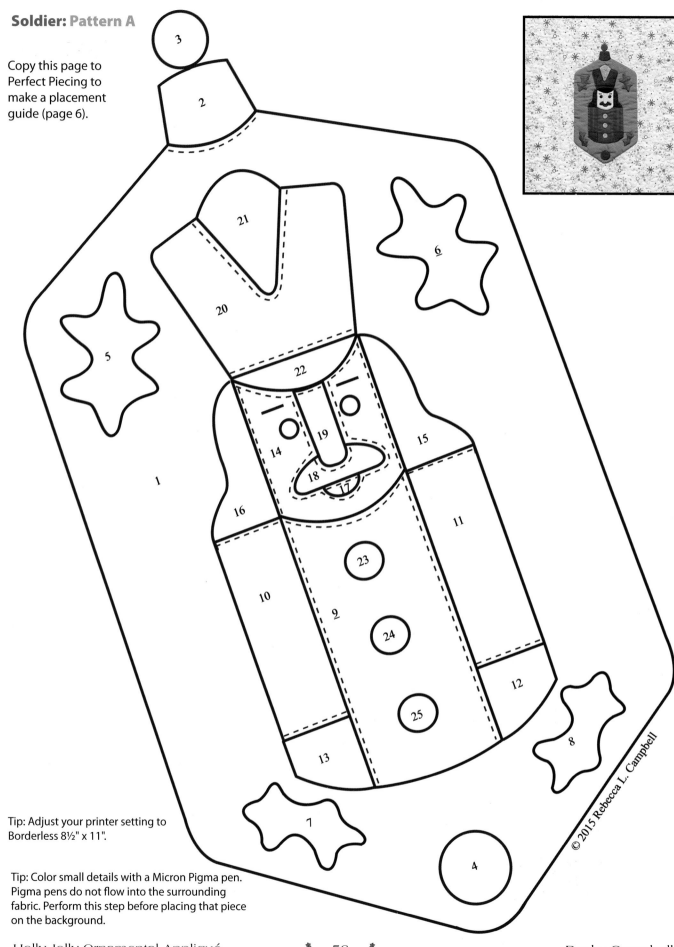

Tip: Adjust your printer setting to
Borderless 8½" x 11".

Tip: Color small details with a Micron Pigma pen.
Pigma pens do not flow into the surrounding
fabric. Perform this step before placing that piece
on the background.

© 2015 Rebecca L. Campbell

Soldier: Pattern B

Copy this page for turned-edge appliqué (page 8), trapunto (page 9), and fusible appliqué (page 9).

------ denotes cutting a generous allowance to extend under another piece.

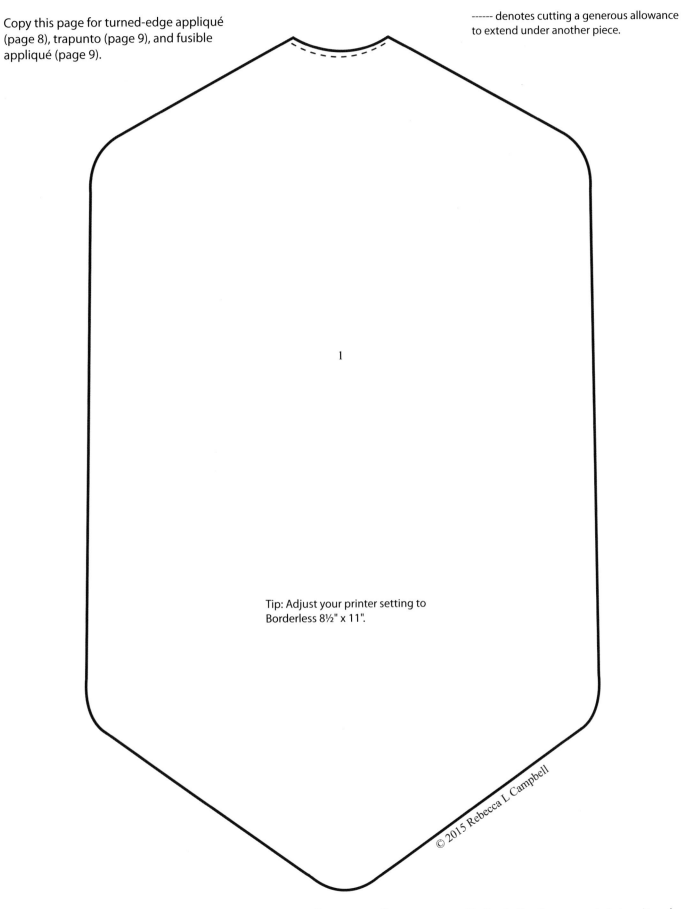

1

Tip: Adjust your printer setting to Borderless 8½" x 11".

© 2015 Rebecca L Campbell

Soldier: Pattern B

Copy this page for turned-edge appliqué (page 8), trapunto (page 9), and fusible appliqué (page 9).

------ denotes cutting a generous allowance to extend under another piece.

Tip: Color small details with a Micron Pigma pen. Pigma pens do not flow into the surrounding fabric. Perform this step before placing that piece on the background.

Tip: Adjust your printer setting to Borderless 8½" x 11".

© 2015 Rebecca L Campbell

Bonus Pattern

Dove Table Runner

Fabric Requirements

Finished size: 68" x 12"
Choose three different fabrics for this table runner.

Red Fabric
  ½ yard for the 3 squares set on point

Print Fabric
  ¾ yard

Green Fabric
  ½ yard, can be a ⅓ yard but that is a bit tight

Binding
  ½ yard

Cutting Instructions

Red Fabric
Cut (3) squares 12½" x 12½" from this piece of fabric, these will be set on point.

Appliqué a dove in the center of both outside squares set on point.

Appliqué a holly leaf in each corner of the center on point square.

Print Fabric
Cut (8) 3½" squares.

Cut (4) 3½" x 6½" rectangles. These will be used at the pointed end of the table runner.

Cut a 45° degree angle on one end of each of the rectangles.

Cut (3) 9¾" squares, cut twice diagonally corner to corner.

These cuts create the (12) side setting triangles.

Green Fabric
Cut (10) 3½" x 3½" squares.

Cut (8) 3½" x 6½" rectangles.

Binding
Cut (5) 2½" strips for binding. Sew strips together end to end with mitered seams.

Please refer to the diagram for fabric placement.

Piece with a ¼" seam.

Assemble into sections which are indicated by the dashed lines.

Join the sections with a ¼" seam.

Please note the pointed ends involve a Y seam, which is easy. Just stop sewing a ¼" away from the cut edge when joining the following seams. Sew the 3½" square to the short side of the pointed piece, stopping a ¼" from the angled end. Add the other pointed piece, sew from the outside point towards the 3½" square stopping a ¼" from the end. You will have stopped right where you stopped before. Sew the short side of the second pointed piece to the other side of the square. Start sewing right where you stopped before, sew all the way to the end of the square.

Layer the pieced top, batting, and backing. Quilt as desired and add the binding. Enjoy!

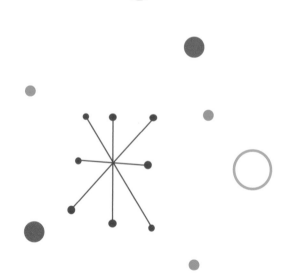

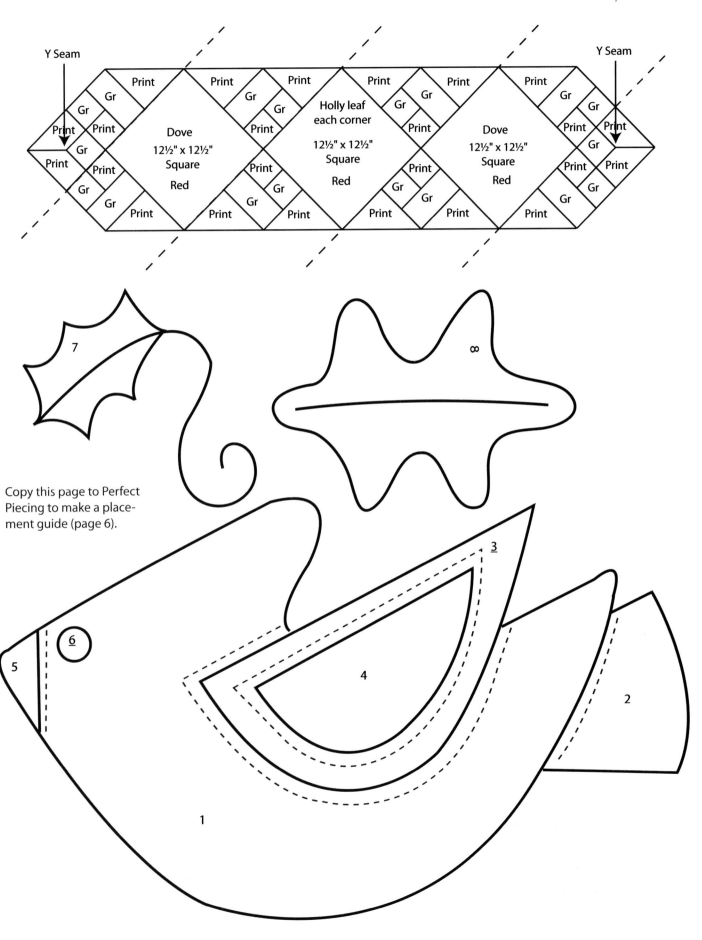

Y Seam

Print
Gr
Gr
Print
Print

Print

Print
Gr
Gr
Print

Print
Gr
Print

Dove
12½" x 12½"
Square

Red

Holly leaf
each corner
12½" x 12½"
Square

Red

Gr
Gr
Print
Print

Gr
Print

Print
Gr
Gr
Print

Print
Gr
Gr
Print

Dove
12½" x 12½"
Square

Red

Gr
Gr
Print
Print

Print
Gr
Print
Print

Y Seam

Print
Print
Gr
Print

Print

Copy this page to Perfect
Piecing to make a place-
ment guide (page 6).

7

8

3

6

5

4

2

1

Dove Table Runner: **Pattern**

Copy this page for turned-edge appliqué
(page 8), trapunto (page 9), and fusible
appliqué (page 9).

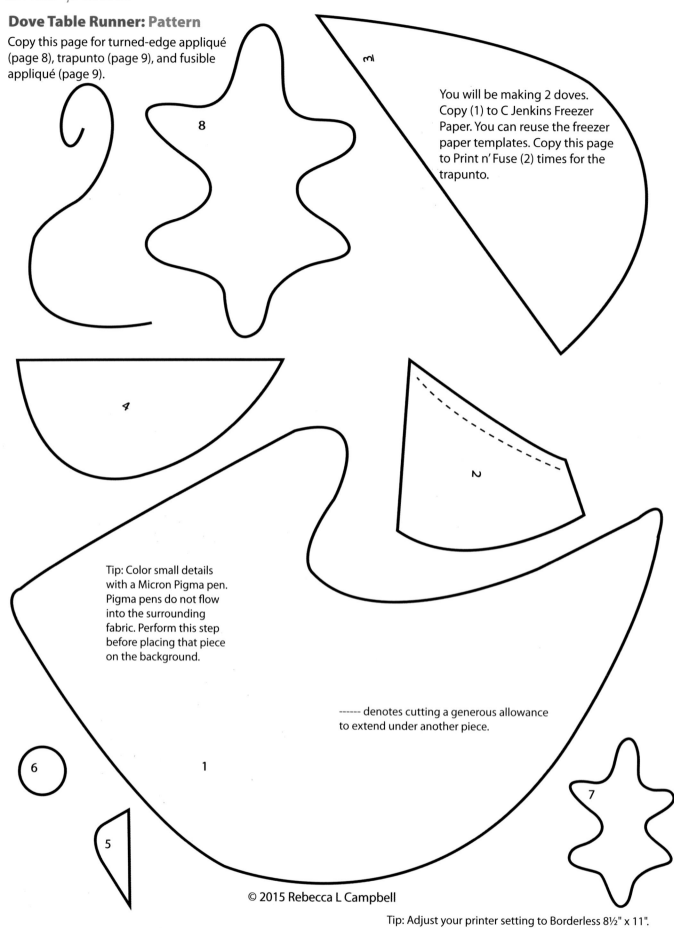

You will be making 2 doves.
Copy (1) to C Jenkins Freezer
Paper. You can reuse the freezer
paper templates. Copy this page
to Print n' Fuse (2) times for the
trapunto.

8

3

4

2

Tip: Color small details
with a Micron Pigma pen.
Pigma pens do not flow
into the surrounding
fabric. Perform this step
before placing that piece
on the background.

------ denotes cutting a generous allowance
to extend under another piece.

6

1

7

5

Tip: Adjust your printer setting to Borderless 8½" x 11".

Holly Jolly Ornamental Appliqué

Becky Campbell

Meet the Author

Becky Campbell

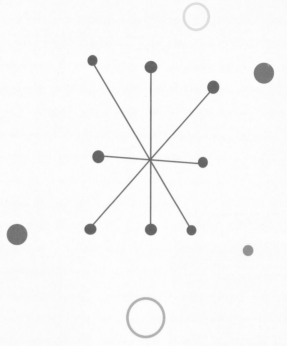

I have been sewing for years. I started making my own clothes, progressed to prom dresses, and then to my wedding dress. I moved on to household items, curtains, pillows—whatever I happened to need. I also decorated our house with all sorts of needlework. Always excited to learn new skills, I took a quilting class in the early 90s. I fell in love. So much to learn, so little time.

I became comfortable making traditional quilts, so I ventured into art quilts. Talk about stretching my skills! There are so many ways to do things, so many products, so much to try.

I discovered that I liked to design products and projects. I designed Sewforever Quilt Storage to provide a better way to store quilts. Then I devised Innovative Appliqué to make appliqué more enjoyable for everyone by increasing accuracy and eliminating time-consuming tasks. In order to be able to share my Innovative Appliqué techniques, I needed original patterns to work with. This led to developing patterns for appliqué.

Quilting is a skill that can always be expanded. Fabric is my paintbrush and imagination my background. The ability to combine these elements into something memorable is always the challenge.

To learn more, visit my website, Facebook page, or contact me directly.

http://www.sewforever.com
http://www.facebook.com/
SewforeverQuiltingbyBeckyCampbell
Becky@sewforever.com

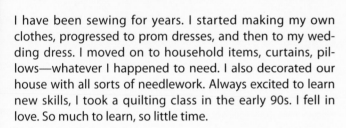

More AQS Books

This is only a small selection of the books available from the American Quilter's Society. AQS books are known worldwide for timely topics, clear writing, beautiful color photos, and accurate illustrations and patterns. The following books are available from your local bookseller, quilt shop, or public library.

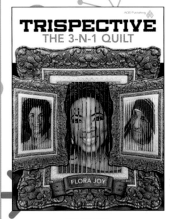

#10281

#10280

#1563

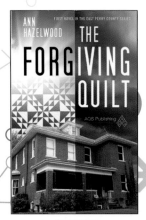

#10279

#10757

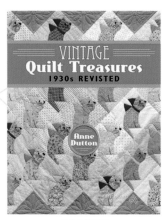

#10277